1,000,000 Books

are available to read at

Forgotten Books

www.ForgottenBooks.com

Read online
Download PDF
Purchase in print

ISBN 978-0-265-26728-8
PIBN 10949871

This book is a reproduction of an important historical work. Forgotten Books uses state-of-the-art technology to digitally reconstruct the work, preserving the original format whilst repairing imperfections present in the aged copy. In rare cases, an imperfection in the original, such as a blemish or missing page, may be replicated in our edition. We do, however, repair the vast majority of imperfections successfully; any imperfections that remain are intentionally left to preserve the state of such historical works.

Forgotten Books is a registered trademark of FB &c Ltd.
Copyright © 2018 FB &c Ltd.
FB &c Ltd, Dalton House, 60 Windsor Avenue, London, SW19 2RR.
Company number 08720141. Registered in England and Wales.

For support please visit www.forgottenbooks.com

1 MONTH OF FREE READING

at

www.ForgottenBooks.com

By purchasing this book you are eligible for one month membership to ForgottenBooks.com, giving you unlimited access to our entire collection of over 1,000,000 titles via our web site and mobile apps.

To claim your free month visit:
www.forgottenbooks.com/free949871

* Offer is valid for 45 days from date of purchase. Terms and conditions apply.

English
Français
Deutsche
Italiano
Español
Português

www.forgottenbooks.com

Mythology Photography **Fiction**
Fishing Christianity **Art** Cooking
Essays Buddhism Freemasonry
Medicine **Biology** Music **Ancient
Egypt** Evolution Carpentry Physics
Dance Geology **Mathematics** Fitness
Shakespeare **Folklore** Yoga Marketing
Confidence Immortality Biographies
Poetry **Psychology** Witchcraft
Electronics Chemistry History **Law**
Accounting **Philosophy** Anthropology
Alchemy Drama Quantum Mechanics
Atheism Sexual Health **Ancient History
Entrepreneurship** Languages Sport
Paleontology Needlework Islam
Metaphysics Investment Archaeology
Parenting Statistics Criminology
Motivational

MINUTES

OF THE

ONE HUNDRED AND SEVENTY-SEVENTH SESSION

OF

Orange Presbytery,

HELD IN THE

CHURCH IN WASHINGTON, N. C.

FAYETTEVILLE:
PRINTED AT THE PRESBYTERIAN JOB OFFICE.
1859

MINUTES

OF

Orange Presbytery.

WASHINGTON, N. C., November 12, 1858.

Presbytery met according to adjournment and was opened with a sermon by Rev. Jacob Doll, Moderator, from Psalm xiv: 2, 3 and 1 Tim. i: 15.

Constituted with prayer.

Present, E. W. Caruthers, D. D., Thomas R. Owen, J. Doll, A. G. Hughes, C. K. Caldwell, S. A. Stanfield, F. N. Whaley, T. G. Wall, J. M. Sherwood, J. M. Kirkpatrick, J. J. Smyth, J. W. Montgomery, J. M. Atkinson, P. H. Dalton and Willis L. Miller, Ministers.

With Mr. William B. Carter, G. T. Baskerville, Wm. C. Bullock, E. Donnell, Richard N. Taylor, Joseph Potts, Dr. D. P. Weir, Stephen Neal, Hugh McCain and C. H. Wiley, Ruling Elders.

Absent, Rev. Messrs. Thomas Lynch, A. Wilson, D. D., Geo. W. Ferrill, James Phillips, D. D., William N. Mebane, Edward Hines, E. C. Bittinger, Archibald Currie, N. Z. Graves, Thomas U. Faucette, Daniel McGilvary and P. A. McMartin.

Rev. John M. Kirkpatrick was chosen Moderator, and Rev. C. K. Caldwell and G. T. Baskerville, Temporary Clerks.

The reading of the Minutes of the last session of Presbytery was dispensed with.

Presbytery then adjourned to meet in the Presbyterian church on to-morrow morning at 9½ o'clock.

Saturday Morning, Nov. 13th, 1858.

Presbytery met according to adjournment and was opened with prayer.

The Minutes of last night's session were read and approved.

A manuscript sermon, by the late Rev. John A. Gretter, on "The Power to Forgive," was presented to Presbytery. This manuscript was referred to a committee consisting of Rev. P. H. Dalton, Rev. A. G. Hughes and Mr. Stephen Neal.

Rev. Simeon Colton, D. D., of Fayetteville Presbytery, Rev. Archibald Baker of Concord Presbytery, and Rev. T. B. Neill of the Presbytery of Cherokee, being present, were invited to sit as corresponding members.

A letter was received from Rev. P. A. McMartin giving satisfactory reasons for absence from the present sessions of Presbytery.

The report of the Committee of Domestic Missions was made the order of the day for Monday at 7 o'clock P. M.

Rev. T. B. Neill presented a certificate of dismission from the Presbytery of Cherokee. After the usual examinations Mr. Neill was received as a member of this Presbytery.

Presbytery then spent an hour in devotional exercises.

Rev. Messrs. Doll, Caruthers and Neal were appointed a committee to prepare a minute in relation to the death of Rev. John H. Pickard.

Dr. D. P. Weir was appointed Treasurer pro tem.

Rev. S. A. Stanfield, Rev. A. G. Hughes and Mr. William C. Bullock were appointed a committee to prepare a minute in relation to the death of Mr. John P. Neal.

Mr. Leonidas H. Yeargan, a member of the church of Raleigh, was introduced to the Presbytery. After an examination on his experimental acquaintance with religion and his views in seeking the gospel ministry, Mr. Yeargan was received by Presbytery as a candidate for the ministry, and placed under the direction of the committee of Education.

Mr. Geo. A. Russell, a licentiate, requested a certificate of dismission to place himself under the care of the Presbytery of Fayetteville. This request was granted.

Inquiry was then made as to the observance of the 3d chapter of the Directory for Public Worship, and the ministers present reported that they had attended to the duty enjoined.

The roll was called and inquiry made respecting the support of the poor. The churches represented, reported that they had no poor supported by the public taxes.

The roll of the churches was called and inquiry made respecting the payment of the travelling expenses of their representatives in Presbytery and Synod.

The committee appointed to organize a church at Mount Airy reported that they had discharged that duty. This report was accepted and adopted.

Another committee, appointed for that purpose, reported that they had organized a church at Roxboro'. This report was accepted and adopted. The church at Roxboro' was then assessed four dollars for the Presbyterial fund.

A committee, appointed for the purpose, reported that they had organized a church in Johnston county by the name of Oakland.

Rev. P. H. Dalton was appointed a committee to organize a church at High Point if the way be open, and also to re-organize the Warrenton church.

Rev. Mr. Ricaud being present was invited to sit as a corresponding member.

Resolved, That all the money contributed to the church extension fund from the 17th day of October, 1857, up to the 17th day of October, 1858, be paid over to the Graham church.

Resolved, That the contributions of our churches from the 17th day of October, 1858, to the 17th day of October, 1859, for church extension, be appropriated to the High Point church, provided that no debt be left resting upon the church, and also that not more than two hundred dollars be required to complete the building.

Rev. E. W. Caruthers, D. D., Rev. T. R. Owen and Mr. Jos. Potts' were appointed a committee on the Minutes of the General Assembly.

The resolution passed at the last meeting of Presbytery, requiring each pastor and stated supply to preach a sermon during each year on the duties of Ruling Elders and Deacons was rescinded.

The two members belonging to Harmony church were directed to enroll their names at Spring Hill church, and the remaining members of Gilead church were directed to enroll their names at Milton.

Resolved, That the next regular meeting of Presbytery be held in the Presbyterian church in Danville, Virginia, to commence on Wednesday before the 3d Sabbath in June, 1859, at 7 o'clock P. M.

The following Ministers and Ruling Elders were nominated as Commissioners to the next General Assembly, viz: J. Doll, Willis L. Miller, J. M. Sherwood and T. G. Wall, Ministers; Dr. D. P. Weir, A. W. Venable, Wm. B. Carter and G. T. Baskerville, Ruling Elders.

The free conversation on the state of religion was made the order of the day for Monday morning at 10 o'clock.

Resolved, That the Agent on Foreign Missions be required to report hereafter only at each spring meeting of Presbytery.

The Presbyterial sermon, by Rev. F. N. Whaley, was postponed until the next meeting of Presbytery.

The Treasurer of Presbytery was ordered to pay the assessment of Synod.

Rev. J. Jones Smyth asked for a dissolution of the pastoral relation existing between himself and the Greensboro' church. The congregation uniting with Mr. Smyth, the request was granted and the Rev. C. K. Caldwell was appointed to declare the church vacant.

Resolved, That the Rev. James Phillips, D. D., be directed to write a letter to the Rev. Daniel McGilvary expressive of the interest that Presbytery feels in the missionary work, and assuring him that their constant prayer to God will be that his life may be spared and his labors abundantly blessed, and that this letter be read before Presbytery on Tuesday morning at 10 o'clock, and that the Presbytery at that time unite in special prayer in his behalf.

Rev. T. G. Wall obtained leave of absence from the remaining sessions of Presbytery.

Presbytery then adjourned to meet on Monday morning at $9\frac{1}{2}$ o'clock.

Closed with prayer.

MONDAY MORNING, November 15, 1858.

Presbytery met according to adjournment and was opened with prayer.

The minutes of Saturday were read and approved.

Mr. John B. Shearer, a licentiate from West Hanover Presbytery, was received under the care of this Presbytery by certificate.

A call from the Chapel Hill church for the pastoral services of Mr. Shearer was then presented to Presbytery. This call being found in order was placed in his hands.

The committee to whom was referred the manuscript sermon by the late Rev. John A. Gretter made the following report, which was accepted and adopted:

"The committee appointed to examine a manuscript sermon by the late Rev. John A. Gretter on 'The Power to Forgive,' beg leave to report, that they have examined the same and find a good deal of difficulty in reading the manuscript, but have learned enough of the sermon to conclude that it is well worth the publishing, provided it can be done. Therefore,

Resolved, That this manuscript be placed in the hands of the Editors of the North Carolina Presbyterian to be published by them in their paper and also in pamphlet form, provided that, in their judgment, they think they can do the author justice in so doing."

The hour for the order of the day at 10 o'clock having arrived, the free conversation on the state of religion was taken up and continued until the hour for public service.

The committee appointed to bring in a minute in relation to the death of Mr. John P. Neal, presented the following, which was accepted and adopted:

"Mr. John P. Neal became a member of the church at Bethesda in the year 1852, was afterwards dismissed to the church at Shiloh, in which he was chosen and acted as Deacon, in 1856 placed himself under the care of Orange Presbytery as a candidate for the gospel ministry, and at the time of the failure of his health in the fall of 1857 was a student of Union Theological Seminary.

He died of consumption on the 18th of September, 1858, in the thirtieth year of his age. His end was calm and peaceful as his life had been humble and consistent.

In each station which he filled, his deportment inspired the confidence of those around him, and was an earnest of usefulness in the ministry of reconciliation. Therefore,

Resolved, 1st. That in this dispensation we are comforted because we believe that our loss is his gain, and because our God did it, and we are admonished to " labor while it is day for the night cometh," and to pray the Lord of the harvest that he may send forth laborers into his harvest.

2nd. That we assure his family and immediate friends that their bereavement is also ours.

3rd. That this minute be published in the North Carolina Presbyterian."

Messrs. C. H. Wiley and Hugh McCain were appointed a committee to examine into the title of the church to a lot of land lying in the county of Randolph, for the purpose of having said title secured.

Presbytery then resumed and concluded the free conversation on the state of religion within our bounds.

The hour for the order of the day having arrived, the report of the Committee of Domestic Missions was presented and accepted.

Pending the discussion on that subject,

Presbytery adjourned until to-morrow morning at $9\frac{1}{2}$ o'clock.

Closed with prayer.

Tuesday Morning, November 16, 1858.

Presbytery met according to adjournment and was opened with prayer.

The minutes of yesterday were read and approved.

A letter was received from Rev. Thomas U. Faucette giving satisfactory reasons for absence from the present sessions of Presbytery.

Rev. John W. Montgomery and Calvin H. Wiley were appointed by Presbytery to attend the Synodical prayer meeting on to-morrow in Newbern.

The Committee on the Minutes of the General Assembly made the following report, which was accepted and adopted:

"The Committee on the Minutes of the General Assembly make the following report, viz:

1. That the resolution of the Assembly appointing the last Thursday in February to be observed as a day of prayer for the baptized children and youth of our church, especially for such as are in colleges, academies and other institutions, be adopted by this Presbytery, and that the observance of said day be recommended to all our churches.

2. That in regard to the Associate Secretaryship of the Board of Domestic Missions (p. 277) your committee did not feel that they were sufficiently acquainted with the facts in the case to recommend any definite action.

3. That on the subject of the monthly concert of prayer for foreign missions recommended by the Assembly (p. 281,) our churches be urged to consider how much the success of all our foreign as well as of our domestic operations depends on prayer; and that the day set apart by general consent and sanctioned by our highest judicatories, be conscientiously and regularly observed.

4. On the subject of the Commentary question, your Committee think that however desirable it may be in some important respects, and however practicable it may be found at some future time, it is inexpedient in the present state of Biblical literature, and therefore would suggest the adoption of the following resolution:

Resolved, That the preparation and publication of a Commentary on the whole Bible, under the direction and by the authority of the highest judicatory in our church, is a matter of so much importance in itself and beset by so many difficulties in the execution, that an immediate procedure with the work would be premature.

5. *Resolved*, That Overture No. 13 on the Demission of the Ministerial Office be answered in the negative by this Presbytery."

Resolved, That the church of High Point, when organized, be supplied with regular monthly preaching by the Pastors of Lexington, Greensboro' and Buffalo, provided their congregations interpose no obstacle, and that the money raised at High Point be a part of the missionary fund of Presbytery.

The committee appointed to prepare a minute in relation to the death of Rev. John H. Pickard made the following report which was accepted and adopted:

"Mr. Pickard was born in Orange county, North Carolina, in March, 1783. He was licensed by the Presbytery of Orange in 1815, and about the year 1816 or 1817, he was ordained and settled as a stated supply at Bethesda church, in Caswell county, North Carolina. He labored statedly in this field, in connection with Stony Creek congregation, for upwards of thirty years. Afterwards, in consequence of failing strength and especially the partial loss of his sight, he labored only occasionally at these churches and occasionally at destitute places in the surrounding country.

In the early part of his ministry, Mr. Pickard labored frequently and successfully as a missionary in several of the adjoining counties.

He was an energetic preacher and a man noted for his humble and fervent piety. A life thus spent ended as might have been expected.

On the 11th day of September, 1858, he peacefully breathed out his life, having frequently during his last illness given expression to a confident hope of a glorious and blessed immortality."

The committee appointed to write to Rev. Daniel McGilvary on behalf of this Presbytery presented the following letter, which was accepted and adopted and the Stated Clerk ordered to forward it to our brother in Bangkok:

"The Orange Presbytery feeling a deep interest in the success of all efforts to spread the knowledge of the truth as it is in Jesus, and believing that an assurance of their constant and unabated affection to you personally and of their continued remembrance of you and the cause in which you are engaged at a throne of grace, might encourage your heart to endure hardness as a good soldier of Jesus Christ, at their present sessions resolved that a letter should be written to you expressing their sympathy with you in your privations and trials, their confidence in your integrity, and their united prayer to the Great Shepherd of Israel that he would bless you and make you a blessing.

Situated as we are, we do not and cannot fully understand your position. We are at home among our families and friends and those speaking our language; you are separated from all the endearments which contribute so much to our earthly comforts, and cut off from intercourse with your fellow-man by a difference of language. We have access to the public ordinances of God's house, and can, as opportunity is afforded us, warn our fellows to flee from the wrath to come; your Sabbaths are comparatively silent and you must see your fellow-man descending to the grave unlighted by the rays of divine truth, and feel your entire impotence to offer help, to throw even a flickering ray of light across the dark valley or point the perishing to the way of life. Brother McGilvary, we sympathize with you most deeply.

You have spent much time already in acquiring some knowledge of language and now find yourself compelled to begin a new one, to learn another alphabet and master a strange speech, and that, too, before you can hope to benefit the immortals perishing around you. This is discouraging, but you are bid to cast your burden on the Lord and are assured that he will sustain you, and your brethren of Orange Presbytery will not cease to pray that God may uphold and comfort and bless you.

But admitting that you were fully prepared to preach the Gospel to the benighted Siamese, you would even then have great trials of faith to endure. The heathen would come to mock, would listen to laugh, and would retire from the place of meeting with the natural enmity of his heart aroused, it may be, to violence. How different is our lot! We can publish salvation and none make us afraid; we can speak of the Man of Mercies and not be threatened with violence. There is this, however, common to us both, that our success is wholly of God; we both have access to the same mercy-seat; both engaged in the same work; both fighting against the same enemies; both led by the same Captain, and both animated by the same Spirit and encouraged by the hope of the same reward. Be of good cheer, therefore, Brother McGilvary, the Lord of Hosts is with you, the God of Jacob is your refuge. Let not the privations you endure, the ceaseless toil to which you are called, the discouragements from want of success by which you may be assailed, nor the opposition of men abate your courage or diminish your hope of ultimate success. He who called you by His grace and separated you unto the gospel of His Son, has promised never to leave you nor forsake you. Compared with this promise the pillared firmament is rotten and its strong foundations weak. Brother McGilvary, run to this refuge, stay yourself on this rock, venture all on this promise. When afraid, make free with your Father's house and hide yourself there, and be assured that your brethren of Orange Presbytery will not cease to give thanks for you and to pray that you may be strengthened with all might in the inner man and that many an ignorant and degraded inhabitant of Siam may, through your instrumentality, emerge out of darkness and be the crown of your rejoicing in the day of the Lord Jesus."

Presbytery then engaged in special prayer for brother McGilvary.

The Committee on the Narrative made a report, which was accepted and a copy of the same ordered to be forwarded to Synod and also to the General Assembly.

Resolved, That Rev. Messrs. S. A. Stanfield, J. W. Montgomery and A. Currie, with Dr. N. M. Roan and R. J. Smith Ruling Elders, be appointed a committee to visit Grier's church on Friday before the second Sabbath in December with a view to heal divisions existing there, if possible, and, if not, report to Presbytery the state of facts.

Rev. John B. Shearer having signified his acceptance of the call from Chapel Hill church, it was

Resolved, That Presbytery hold an adjourned meeting at Chapel Hill on Friday before the first Sabbath in February at 7 o'clock P. M., with a view to his ordination and installation as Pastor of that church.

1. The Moderator to propose the constitutional questions and make the ordination prayer.

2. Rev. J. M. Atkinson to preach the ordination sermon—Rev. A. G. Hughes his alternate.

3. Rev. J. M. Sherwood to charge the Minister—Rev. A. Wilson D. D., his alternate.

4. Rev. S. A. Stanfield to charge the people and Rev. A. Currie his alternate.

Rom. viii: 1 was assigned to Mr. Shearer as the subject for his trial sermon.

The following commissioners were elected to the next General Assembly, viz: Ministers J. Doll with W. L. Miller alternate, and J. M. Sherwood with T. G. Wall alternate ; Ruling Elders Dr. D. P. Weir with G. T. Baskerville alternate, William B. Carter with A. W. Venable alternate.

Resolved, That when Presbytery adjourns, it will adjourn to meet in Newbern during the sessions of Synod at the call of the Moderator.

Resolved, That the thanks of this Presbytery be tendered to the citizens of Washington for their hospitality to the members of this body, and to the officers of the Methodist Episcopal and Baptist Churches for the use of their houses of worship during this meeting, and the pastors of these churches be requested to read this resolution from their pulpits.

Presbytery then adjourned to meet in Newbern at the call of the Moderator.

Closed with singing, prayer and the Apostolic benediction.

J. DOLL, *Stated Clerk.*

MINUTES

OF

The Adjourned Meeting.

NEWBERN, N. C., November 18, 2858.

Presbytery met according to adjournment at the call of the Moderator and was opened with prayer.

The Committee of Domestic Missions nominated the following list of Supplies, which was accepted and adopted, viz:

Rev. C. K. Caldwell	2 Sabbaths at	High Point.
" C. H. Wiley	2 "	" "
" E. W. Caruthers, D. D.	3 "	" Long's Mills.
" J. Doll	1 "	" Leaksville.
" J. M. Kirkpatrick	1 "	" "
" D. E. Jordan	1 "	" "
" S. A. Stanfield	1 "	" "
" A. G. Hughes	1 "	" Haywood.
" J. Phillips, D. D.	1 "	" "
" P. A. McMartin	2 "	" Stony Creek.
" E. H. Harding	1 "	" Roxboro'.
" E. Hines	Roxboro' at discretion.
" Charles Phillips	1 Sabbath at	Pittsboro'.
" W. L. Miller	1 "	" "
" W. L. Miller	1 "	" Haywood.
" J. B. Shearer	1 "	" Pittsboro'.
" J. B. Shearer	1 "	" Station.
" A. Wilson, D. D.	1 "	" Lexington.
" P. H. Dalton,	1 "	" Lexington.
" Thomas R. Owen	1 "	" Louisburg.
" J. M. Sherwood	1 "	" discretion.

Rev. J. J. Smyth 1 Sab. at Hillsdale and 1 at Mt. Airy.
" J. W. Montgomery - - 1 Sabbath at Mt. Airy.
" F. N. Whaley - - - 1 " " Warrenton.
" T. G. Wall 1 Sab. at Kinston and 1 Sab. at discretion.

Presbytery then adjourned to meet at Chapel Hill on Friday before the first Sabbath in February, 1859, at 7 o'clock P. M.

Closed with prayer.

J. DOLL, *Stated Clerk.*

CPSIA information can be obtained
at www.ICGtesting.com
Printed in the USA
LVHW080518271118
598291LV00012BA/1107/P